BIENNIAL: POEMS

BIENNIAL: POEMS

Michael Joyce

BLAZEVOX[BOOKS]
Buffalo, New York

Biennial: poems
by Michael Joyce
Copyright © 2015

Published by BlazeVOX [books]

All rights reserved. No part of this book may be reproduced without
the publisher's written permission, except for brief quotations in reviews.

Printed in the United States of America

Interior design, cover design and typesetting by Geoffrey Gatza
Cover Art by Michael Joyce

First Edition
ISBN: 978-1-60964-215-0
Library of Congress Control Number: 2015937799

BlazeVOX [books]
131 Euclid Ave
Kenmore, NY 14217

Editor@blazevox.org

publisher of weird little books

BlazeVOX [books]

blazevox.org

21 20 19 18 17 16 15 14 13 12 01 02 03 04 05 06 07 08 09 10

BlazeVOX

Acknowledgments

The epigraph to the preface is from Lawrence Weschler's, *Seeing Is Forgetting the Name of the Thing One Sees Expanded Edition, Over Thirty Years of Conversations with Robert Irwin*, University of California Press, and I am grateful to the press for confirming that it represents fair use. The lines, which appear on pages 71 and 73 in my edition, are not in verse form in the original.

Thanks, hurrah and rockets to Geoffrey Gatza, publisher, editor, poet, novelist, playwright, visual artist, and chef, named one of the Top 200 Advocates for American Poetry by *The Huffington Post* in 2013, and who has prevailed despite the obstacles and naysayers.

Thanks also to Andrew Axel, Kasia Bazarnik, Hannah Berkin-Harper, Charles Bernstein, Lily Bernstein, Muriel Bruttin, Karmen Buckey, Christina Carozza, Hélène Cixous, Danielle Cliche, Teresa Croke, Andrew Culbreth, Walter Cybulski, Maria Engberg, John Enright, Zenon Fajfer, Meghan Feldmeier, Emily Finney, Don Foresta, Andy Goodnow, Max Herman, Roy Hudson, Jane Gregory, Elayne Janiak, Gilbert Martha Joyce, Gabriella Kardos, Marianne Kardos, Julie Louis, Piotr Marecki, Paul Meshejian, Dylan Moon, Grace Moon, Rose Noel Moon, Grace Ndiritu, Martha Petry, Dominique Peysson, Camilla Pfeiffer, Mariusz Pisarski, Alex Raz, Robert Ronan, Elizabeth Rowland, Daria Schieferstein, Leonard Schwartz, Allen Shelton, Linda Tuttle, Zijun Clivia Wang, as well as Eamon, Jeremiah, and all the others (t)here for these days.

For Tom.

With love to Carolyn, she of all my days and nights.

This book is dedicated to Talulla Thomas Joyce, she who brought life to these days:

> Tuilelaith, dubbed little one,
> dear first blossom of spring,
> Blume des Elsass, blue-eyed
> Bohanphrionsa beag
> of all the equinoctial generations
> on this earth and in the heavens.

Introduction

"I found a certain strength in sustaining
over a period of time
my attention on a single point.

"I embarked on two years of painting
those paintings
two lines on each canvas
and at the end of two years
there were ten of them...
a total of twenty lines
over a period of two years.

"There was no separation
between me
and those paintings."

Robert Irwin from *"seeing is forgetting the name of the thing one sees"*

One day in April 2012, I read the lines above and decided to write two years of two line poems. There was nothing special about that particular day, save that I had read what Robert Irwin said about what he did and thought about what might be the equivalent discipline for a poet. To have written only ten couplets during these two years might have been that, but only had they, like Irwin's paintings, condensed into themselves innumerable lines and erasures in the moments of those years. It is possible that some readers might find that only ten (or fewer) of the poems that follow emerge as that kind of distillation from what seems otherwise precipitate. There are times when I feel that only very few of these poems accomplish what I wanted, but the problem is that from reading to reading which ones these are shifts in my estimation.

"What I wanted" is, of course, itself problematic. First was to come as close to achieving in the poems Irwin's sense of there being no separation between himself and his paintings. Which is to say, I think, that I wanted to learn the different ways that lines in poems work on different days to different purposes. I think some of these achieve that. Others strike me as mere journal entries or quotidian observation, but which ones these are likewise shift in my estimation.

Along the way events, including the events of these poems themselves, altered the project. A poppy noticed one day showed itself more clearly the next. A series of walks along a marsh near the Gironde took on a quality of bilingual narrative, doubling the sense of two lines. There were more serious events of course. My brother died, my granddaughter was born, others die, are born, and marry, a scare sent me to the cardiac unit of the hospital, students came and went, anniversaries and holidays were marked, I traveled to Poland, Sweden, and France, birds too came and went outside our window, deer moved through the yard, the Hudson flowed back and forth before us in shifting light. The two years unwound and then the project ended, a total of 731 short poems over two years plus one day. I wrote this invocation.

BIENNIAL: POEMS

4.3.12

To start with two lines then in black and white
and continue to see a way in them.

4.4.12

Across the street the dog barks at something beyond
the line demarcated by the invisible electric fence

4.5.12

How to ease these excitements of mind
the crow now gone mute, the morning empty

4.6.12

They talk after breakfast in the room below
while I have slipped away to this.

4.7.12

Seeking to widen the horizon that divides itself
between what is called the true and what the visible

4.8.12

Ēostre comes up the hill this morning in her holiday attire:
platinum hair over striped chemise, wobbly on high heels

4.9.12

In the blur the far-off figure
fading or coming into view

4.10.12

My mother died this day three decades ago,
how much more here can I be than this moment?

4.11.12

Still life: white brick rectangle of Breuer's Ferry House
afloat against a backdrop of dark fir and cedar.

4.12.12

The patient blink of the cursor a mark now that the irrevocable
can be reversed by something less tactile than erasure was once.

4.13.12

settles despite complaint
poem (rain)   against itself

4.14.12

Curiosity an irritation, the wayward, the way words
come to you and go away a narrative, a way to go

4.15.12

The space between seen differently each day, or so I wrote before
my assault makes the trapped wasp thrash between the panes

4.16.12

this awaiting, this
momentary calm

4.17.12

The first day of an illness as if setting out on a journey
hoping to meet yourself upon the way.

4.18.12

desire destabilizes form in its longing
what flower shall I name as an instance?

4.19.12

Two women laughing at the intersection outside,
I go to the window but do not see them.

4.20.12

Add a parenthesis and the word, this, is
housekeeping, the house where I live

4.21.12

Weekend noise of machines *contra naturam*
retracing imperceptible margins

4.22.12

Begin with an article, an action follows
the stone amulets in my pocket I keep losing

4.23.12

A riddle is a form for this difference:
is what a fast slows a thing?

4.24.12

A carved stone bear, its back arched, an invoice, a blue cloth for polishing a screen. "Yeats as list maker," P. Muldoon. "what life isn't daily…what poetry isn't everyday?" B. Mayer.

4.25.12

Such silence
le bien-être

4.26.12

I think myself
alone here in my body.

4.27.12

Here the heart of things
is the heart of things

4.28.12

vagrant silk of the dreamer's dissilience
issues forth from the hospital night

4.29.12

my resurrection spent
in stage business

4.30.12

Qu'est-ce qui s'est passé? marks that
which puts both itself and what is in question

5.1.12

a light rain garlands the lilacs
the girls once wove into crowns

5.2.12

grey Providence
a siren disappears into its own echo

5.3.12

maiden cellist's lip *coll'arco*, smile suppressed,
whilst she waits to pluck the satyr's score

5.4.12

a week exactly after a walk-through of his own passing
he remarks his dead father's birthday

5.5.12

the here, the the, this this, the mark of this inescapable rhythm that
Creeley and Basho both trod better long before

5.6.12

tell how far are
you here where you are

5.7.12

nowhere yet the lack of separation; I recall a photograph
placid pewter sea and overcast, horizon's bead a solder flux

5.8.12

he bid me come
the man on the shore

5.9.12

in the parable the servant waits outside the kitchen in the shade of the thin tree in the courtyard
its dark pool already shrinking under the sun's ascent, shadow swallowed into its vortex

5.10.12

last night and this morning
come differently to a man who has sons

5.11.12

abidance and collimation
inflected, interstitial light

5.12.12

It is not true to say I have walked back to smooth the stones along this path before going on
for here are neither path nor stones, nor a before or after moving

5.13.12

four copies of a journal publishing three poems arrive
where they lay on the table, crisp and as yet unread

5.14.12

as we sleep, houses– and in storms, trees– according to Tranströmer,
wander from their places, for a time distorting this platted village

5.15.12

he peers into the screen as if a well
your name scribbling itself upon its surface

5.16.12

ache of dawn follows the clamoring of birds
rain lingering, moan of a long train resounding

5.17.12

deformation itself a pattern discovered
décollage and appliqué this much alike

5.18.12

stone drill rattles on iron treads
iron pterodactyl pecking bedrock

5.19.12

is this involute rhythm a form of me
or the metric of a studied symmetry

5.20.12

today we commence in sunlight
leçon: tous se termine

5.21.12

emptied caravanserai
deserted carnevale

5.22.12

Taihao, fashioned from baby's first cut hair, Shuxu, Wang Xizhi's rat whisker landscape brush,
Shanma, of mountain horse mane, Dong Langmao, winter wolf, good for forming chrysanthemums

5.23.12

a name in a poem Andrew said
carries great weight with it

5.24.12

in the morning *Times* comes word
American poetry has changed overnight

5.25.12

mourning
dove, dove, dove

5.26.12

not quite able to awake after stupid dreams
unable to fold a fabric squarely, still there on return

5.27.12

the faces behind the headlights along the highway at midnight remain
now that the early morning fog has dissipated, lovers gone home

5.28.12

cellphone as an ontological device, txt to&from a body not one's own,
in service of a constructed self, future a fleeting transcription, lost

5.29.12

alone with one's ambitions
as if in a room of strangers

5.30.12

distant motor ceases
finch song remains

5.31.12

a lone poppy this spring
not visible from here

6.1.12

the red of it
seen today

6.2.12

once long ago watching sky writing disperse behind a twisting bi-plane,
hand to brow a visor against the glare, Jones Beach windless below

6.3.12

empty thump of car doors as the church-goers disembark
then make their way in sunlight to enter the wooden ark

6.4.12

where have I gone I ask at the station
the platform is empty, sky threatening

6.5.12

draw a line from nowhere to here
then another, parallel, at a distance following logically from the first

6.6.12

a rail ticket to a far shore comes from SNCF in an email
I would be as a nun dedicating her morning to absence

6.7.12

wait quietly for
the hour to pass

6.8.12

sweeps the stone floor then sweeps it again
two separate acts for the one who attends

6.9.12

in her dream she says she discovers what seems an unknown fact:
that one can be with her and at the same time be somewhere else

6.10.12

where doubt locates itself is
what differs this from prayer

6.11.12

A day that begins backwards continues so throughout:
lines written on the previous day's account debit *decollage horaire*

6.12.12

Au lit like Proust, but in the wrong district and a century after, in a two star hotel
Plus heureux however, even waking at six to that number and its doubles

6.13.12

The tourists hurry along the Seine in the in-between hour through cold rain,
Notre Dame dark, bullies taunt one another between bank and *bateau-mouche*

6.14.12

Rabbi on a bicycle, son in a basket, along rue Saint Paul
Clack of heels on the cobblestone collonade of rue du Prévôt

6.15.12

Wake again trying to recall
how to tend to one self

6.16.12

After a thump and the howl the plump woman in pink lay on the rainy pavement of Rue Rivoli,
the taxi driver argued his innocence in the night, the blond witness having crossed to shriek at him.

6.17.12

Dark-eyed Ariane, the "utterly pure," presides behind the bar along Parmentier
squeezing orange juice and making *café crème* for her *équipe* of brusque devotees

6.18.12

angry for another
anger for oneself

6.19.12

The afternoon an expanse between appetite and hunger
walking in the dust and sunshine of Brooklyn piers

6.20.12

upriver awaiting the boat to nowhere, the tide favorable,
offering brunch to the aging sailor and his bride

6.21.12

outside the heat
no escaping the heat

6.22.12

dream a damp cavern beneath a stone walkway through which chinks of sky and sunlight:
life, I knew, my heart filled with gratitude and loss in witness of even these few fragments

6.23.12

rake's wave pattern
adds back the sea

6.24.12

a day lost in the arithmetic
solstice as simple as that

6.25.12

A case of mistaken identity: Joe Gould's pages, not Joe Brainard's, in Estlin's notebooks
among the daily studies of Marion I catalogued that summer in the Patchin Place attic

6.26.12

it is impossible to ready everything
for where we are eventually going

6.27.12

river gilt in last night's twilight through a thin curtain of bamboo,
then just beyond the cedar fence a fawn haunch passes slowly below

6.28.12

the silence of animals
no different than this

6.29.12

staticky Telemann for two clarinets as I wait on hold
until a woman in Maharashtra wishes me good morning

6.30.12

for the djinn of vestibules
the day is a garden

7.1.12

In my brother's poem our mother celebrated New Year's on her birthday in July before we were born
Now 30 years after she died, she waves from *en liten segelbåt* this *sommarmorgon* on Lake Malaren

7.2.12

Duncan's question of where the sun is vis à vis each poem
vivid here this Swedish morning, distant shore through trees

7.3.12

In the *rossengården* the black-capped *parus major* flit among the columns
snatching crumbs among the woven reeds of wicker armchairs

7.4.12

What— and by or to what— are these birds called
who put the light to sleep these hours after midnight?

7.5.12

sommormorgon light floods the edges of the shades at four a.m.
and I don my sleep mask to return *till drömmen maskeraden*

7.6.12

the scent of a lioness lingers
among the sleeping fig trees

7.7.12

puts words before his desires, as on an altar
or the way the stitch domesticates the dithyramb

7.8.12

all night the rain in the *cour intérieure* upon the green tables
a Swedish perturbation spinning southward *sur L'Île-de-France*

7.9.12

along the Gironde the mourning doves sing their low desire in Charentaise
as a choir of ten thousand *hélianthes* turn their faces *vers le crescendo du matin*

7.10.12

swallows swoop and twist in the garden courtyard after rain
the buzz of a moto unraveling the morning along the *estuaire*

7.11.12

Port-Maubert to Royon and back in a crooked line at 00:31 a.m.
the creatures in order: hedgehog, owl, hawk, two rabbits, two cats, lone fox

7.12.12

Think to draw a line, top to bottom, upon the travelogue,
then live on either side of the place this mirror describes

7.13.12

Friday *le treizième*
Bon chance everyone

7.14.12

Deux grands cigognes circle the bull *en point* in the field on the edge
of the marsh near *La Grange des Marais* this holiday morning

7.15.12

juste avant minuit
mugit le silence

just before midnight
the silence roars

7.16.12

Dome of blue serene above the reeds of the *marais*
at the end of the *chemin* yawns the river's expanse

7.17.12

wrens stitch the canebrake along the levee
against which the passer-by is a shadow

7.18.12

almost twist an ankle watching the stork walk
regally through new mown hay then soar away

7.19.12

under the rain the grisaille on the far off shore
salt scent of the sea rides the incoming tide

7.20.12

a trio of gendarmes dig a trench in the sand
with blue plastic shovels, *c'est vrai*

7.21.12

une lacune déguisée
yet no dream

7.22.12

la chauve-souris, the bat circles then disappears,
yet I still swat at it, still sitting blindly here

7.23.12

the marsh grass is borderless
except for the river and the fence

le pâturin des marais sont sans frontière
hors du fleuve et la barrière

7.24.12

something is happening
the fishermen leave port

choses bougent au-delà
les pêcheurs quittent le port

7.25.12

out there somewhere
I still walk

quelque part je
marche toujours

7.26.12

at 38,000 feet the captain
sleeps on his side beside me

7.27.12

back here where I am
no longer myself

7.28.12

in the thick of
another river

7.29.12

sunday
undone

7.30.12

coppery green curve of the mallard
at dawn upon the pewter pool

7.31.12

after the drive I swim alone
in the turquoise motel pool

8.1.12

Somali women in multicolored *diracs* along Grant Street, Buffalo, NY
clutch wide-eyed children to their hips and wait for the number three bus

8.2.12

native Irish-American son navigates formerly Italian
Burmese neighborhoods of his home town via GPS

8.3.12

we tire early and wake the same
into the ambiguity of dawn

8.4.12

along the way I have lost
the line I have found

8.5.12

summer an elsewhere
inside a chilled box

8.6.12

chickory flower lies low
to avoid the blade

8.7.12

again the rhythm that overtakes these lines makes a monotony of them
on his mind a skate blade along ice, the sweat and echo of it, frost then blue

8.8.12

how the river lifts itself
seen where the road ends

8.9.12

writing to great men
pretending to be such

8.10.12

muffled clusters
of distant fireworks

8.11.12

Saturday silence descending into the river town full of tourists
seen from the air conditioned remove of the slow moving sedan

8.12.12

"to linger and keep a while"
at the edge of the morrow

8.13.12

cricket in the damp air sings
mere fact of the morning

8.14.12

I write of curry fish, stir-fried rice noodles, radicchio stewed in coconut milk
an instance of "the time and space that defines our connection," or so he replies

8.15.12

approaching Duchamp's "point of indifference"
where the thing can be seen for itself

8.16.12

Cricket song along *la rivière Richelieu*
Against the rush of traffic *sur la rue*

8.17.12

drunk with excess
choke in your bile

soûl avec l'excès
étouffe dans ta bile

8.18.12

in the silence of *le coin rond*, or what we would call the elbow of the river,
a woman's voice sounds beyond the wall *qui sépare ces balcons*

8.19.12

line lost, crow caw
at summer end

8.20.12

forgotten, the poem appears
Sleepless beyond midnight

8.21.12

You would think it might have struck me well before now that what constitutes a line for the present purpose isn't determined by the margins or, for that matter, by the varieties of prosodic inevitability— whether haiku-like or the idiosyncratic, but nonetheless predictable, lyric— that I've tried without success to shake free of here, the frustration of failing to find what— against what he called "the mossiness of Mallarmé"— Eliot found in Pound's appropriation of the "form and measure… of Peire Vidal's *'Ab l'alen tir vas me l'aire'*" of which EP insisted it was "fit only to be sung, and is not to be spoken."

All of that seems distant, their concerns alien to how, having come late to it, I have for six years now slowly taken on both the practice and profession of what filled their London lives with such insistence; for if this—that is, these "lines" or the project entire— enacts a steady investigation into poetics, it gives way before the sudden appearance of hooped ripples upon the shallows of the river at dusk—feeding fish or insects settling, or the two at once— beneath the waxing crescent moon.

8.22.12

there along the shore, here a long hour
draws close the line between them

8.23.12

some mornings as I walk I am aware of the self there, a young prince hitching a ride in my body,
his closed carriage gliding serene as a steadicam just below the diaphragm at the Manipura chakra

8.24.12

in the silence
of the poem

8.25.12

dull clink of stone masons' hammers
low talk in Spanish *a lo largo de la muro*

8.26.12

why suppose death comprises
an instant more than does a life

8.27.12

"Self worried –using /handiwork helped/relieve tension"
my father wrote in his daybook thirty years ago this day

8.28.12

outside the strip-mall cafe in the steamy advance of the storm
a lone man sitting at a table in the sun over iced coffee

8.29.12

mere occasion no occasion
what is happening without

8.30.12

emptiness of the blue moon
rising between dark boughs

8.31.12

perhaps I should accept
this rhythm as my own

9.1.12

spectres of dead flowers piled upon a high shelf
anthology of our days become thanatology's decor

9.2.12

waiting for what
comes next

9.3.12

chemical or barometric the change of mood descends
sullen mystery lasting night, morning, and half afternoon

9.4.12

inside the house outside the rain
outside the house inside the rain

9.5.12

the lost day was earlier, but where?
crows settling after the cutting

9.6.12

a soft fog clings to the low hills downriver between Cedar Cliff and Danskammer
a flock of sparrows corkscrews from the bittersweet bush, returning as the grey walker passes

9.7.12

Clivia, the Kaffir lily, Camilla, a woman warrior
misspoke flowers east and west, rain like soft applause

9.8.12

at the edge of the latest tempest I plot my resentments, searching etymologies and concordances
of flowers, communicating my findings to distant relations and pupils linked by telephone and texts

9.9.12

Sunday noon, the front passed, the box fan rattles in the window
as the congregants, having serenaded the departing organist, drive off

9.10.12

what risk is this
cleaving, what advance?

9.11.12

does he burn, someone asks
in a dream before sleeping

9.12.12

consider these days as a series
of questions posed to a shadow

9.13.12

what we are left with is the ellipsis
where what was marked remains undone

9.14.12

the widowed sister and the younger son
each speak of dinners as if communion

9.15.12

he sails away there
before her eyes

9.16.12

the hammers of the heart
sound deep within my ear

9.17.12

this day or another given
over to the coming rain

9.18.12

inescapable phenotypic rhythm
locked or lodged in his genotype

9.19.12

the poem the program recovered after the power failure
would not have been lost to a poet with a trained memory

9.20.12

mist on the misbegotten lake
a squadron of mowers swarms toward

9.21.12

above Canajoharie the long low valleys
pool into a light that turns back centuries

9.22.12

rough breathing of the sleeping woman
a silent skiff cast forth close to shore

9.23.12

Finally home, we layer the blankets against the autumn chill
willing sleep upon us like the drowning man the waves' lamellae

9.24.12

it isn't necessary to specify the leaf
that falls beneath an imaginary bower

9.25.12

I caught this day before it turned
something other than what it was

9.26.12

autumn fallen in a sodden lump this morning, yard chimes sounding the wind the rain rides upon
while two blocks away the train comes in and out of the station as if through a stone canyon

9.27.12

The poet's long hair and soft
voice like a banked fire igniting

9.28.12

drip upon the aluminum gutter *Tewehigan,* Algonquin for drum's first syllable
aspirated becomes an onomatopoetic heartbeat, *Croíbhualadh* among our clan

9.29.12

awakened from a dream that does not end yet staggering on
beneath a lowering sky over leaf tatter upon the sodden lawn

9.30.12

not some
no where

10.1.12

broidered veil of tinkling bells
trails the recurrent October winds

10.2.12

birthday wish for a former lover
forlorn dispatch upon a rainy day

10.3.12

 "underlying script" belies
a lost night's dreaming

10.4.12

god god god god, a dull prayer softly
thudding against the mind's disquiet

10.5.12

amid night,
forget fullness

10.6.12

she is planting next spring's bulbs before breaking her fast while I write likewise,
our marriage wrought of what can be done before giving way to graver measures

10.7.12

smell of onions in a broth of squash
and root vegetables wafts from below

10.8.12

I told the boy who asked if I was still writing
these lines that I had not written as yet

10.9.12

dogs barking and the nail gun
play out an afternoon crucifixion

10.10.12

against the great lies of politics
a mind lost in updates

10.11.12

joyous ferocity springs unseen, the gleam
of the leopard dark as the cave he's within

10.12.12

timidly he confesses his loneliness,
pardon? you're breaking up, the reply

10.13.12

This season's first creak of the furnace sets the studs groaning beyond the lath;
past its uninsulated cavity a hard frost coats the silver auto and the herb bed

10.14.12

what could you think
has happened to you

10.15.12

in the darkness of space the daredevil tumbles
through the blue to the desert below

10.16.12

what do you not love of this world? Consider, for instance, how the low waves
score the garnet bay where it is held in the compass of a saffron dusted shore

10.17.12

confessing he wakes most days feeling a failure, the poet
is thought to need counsel beyond what the poem offers

10.18.12

somewhere in the night the unavoidable fall
from which the sleeper awakes unconvinced

quelque part dans la nuit vient la chute incontournable
à partir de laquelle le dormeur se réveille pas convaincu

10.19.12

still trembling at day's end
the leaves and their witness

10.20.12

along the Shawangunks down through the lowlands then back up past Ashoken
into the Catskills toward Phoenicia, a gold thread drawn through purple cloth

10.21.12

no one can tell
any one thing

10.22.12

time turned politic, night's motion
yields to morning without a second

10.23.12

at the edge of rain in the early afternoon
leaf scent of a six year ago Paris autumn

10.24.12

sometimes the ghost of a line appears
a dry creek beneath the traceless clay

10.25.12

assailed by the worries one chooses,
the choices themselves among them

10.26.12

tending to what has gone before, the list
of lost words: dried, bed, earth, worm

10.27.12

a rotational force nears landfall
on a muted television above the bar

10.28.12

once again erecting the royal platform in the cellar
where we will sit if the roof blows off in the tempest

10.29.12

exultation of the storm like the death of a parent:
I am living now, the wind says and there is no reply

10.30.12

in the dull and sullen grey of afternoon midst desultory gusts
the tourists come to gape upon the remnants of the flood wrack

10.31.12

The dead return to the valley although the tunnels remain flooded
candles flickering as the few children make their way among them

11.1.12

las figuras pintada del Día de los Muertos en la mesa del banqueto
bang their forks against the planks and demand morsels of flesh

11.2.12

grey to grey a relay
the day's monotony

11.3.12

sparse herd of dun deer graze on the upslope beyond the meadow where
the angus cattle are arrayed, winter fur already bristling their black flanks

11.4.12

Remembers the poem as if someone waiting for him
she waving there along a siding just beyond the station

11.5.12

Through desperate dreams pursuing the road beneath this one
the line on the form where one enters the missing information.

11.6.12

the day begins and in its shadows
we elect to become ourselves

11.7.12

The gusts rustle through the last unstripped maple,
neither intentional utterance, nor whisper nor hiss

11.8.12

once thought each of these eves an omen
years forming themselves in their turning

11.9.12

a confetti of candied fennel seeds and a hoop of changing colored LEDs
mark the meridian along each of the twelve ways to approach heaven

11.10.12

the bare blue-grey forests of the Berkshires shoulders veiled this morning
higher ridges sun-stippled above a faint blush of bittersweet and winterberry

11.11.12

as the grip of the malady slowly lets go and the torpor recedes, the return of who I think I am
presents itself as a distant event befalling an unknown someone somewhere I once have been

11.12.12

by definition this accident was not
among the things he had planned

11.13.12

train horn complaining in the grey of late morning
grunt from the damp pavement, forlorn bells beyond

11.14.12

just before Spuyten Duyvil fiery copper foil of the early sunset
between the plum dark Palisades and a bank of cinereal clouds

11.15.12

a day that leaves no mark
save a weary pummeling

11.16.12

Khayyám's parallels notwithstanding
these lines veer no nearer one another

11.17.12

comes from
under a cloud

11.18.12

when I was young I would have thought it something to go to the city and back in one day
a walk through Cobble Hill Saturday night streets, two bottles of wine, the train ride home

11.19.12

Going forth by day from Fratelli's to Récollets, Niamh swimming among the Asrais
and a memory of August in a storm of golden threads, the hexaphonic guitar like rain

11.20.12

at a certain age one chooses to wake rather than simply waking
pushing above the surface of the wave rather than delivered to the shore

11.21.12

The wounded ones grunt and doze in the parsonage parlor
while in the kitchen chirping strangers beat pastry into leather

11.22.12

sun streams through the breakfast room of the motel
bleaching the earnest faces of the morning news hosts

11.23.12

They lay, a fraternal pieta against the kitchen cabinets, the one who fell grey,
the one who caught him splayed, wide-eyed and incredulous in shock and pain

11.24.12

These days annually lost within each other, the feast day seeming a Sunday,
Friday a premature Saturday, the latter unmarked except by the stream of traffic

11.25.12

A day of dalliance
real and imagined

11.26.12

glib entry giving way to a change of day
the merely calendrical suddenly architectonic

11.27.12

white couple at the Red Rooster on Lennox Ave,
festive in Harlem among Swedes at the Fall Gasque

11.28.12

full moon in Gemini helplessly descending since noon
one third of the way toward midnight's waning gibbous

11.29.12

a waiting
her return

11.30.12

In the masquerade of myself I play the part
of me that cannot meet himself in the eye

12.1.12

one bracketed by a doubled fullness that riddles
what it and two-to-four plus six divide but not five

12.2.12

lost double of
solitary (de)vice

12.3.12

Two lines here erased in a prior swipe of light no palimpsest
thoughts of incarnation and the fall both vanishing in a blue blink

12.4.12

Imagine the figure of her no longer there rising in the dim of this still-dark morning
or him gone from the chair where he sits at the end of an otherwise routine evening

12.5.12

Writes the beginning of a story, "judgment-in-flux,
as you say," someone says to him, paraphrasing

12.6.12

Empty pleasures of the cavalcade pall
yet still the horseless rider plods on

12.7.12

Ni saltimbanquerie nor saltimbanquesque a word in either language to the best of his knowledge
yet how else describe a day that begins with walking into walls and ends in carnal dégringolade?

12.8.12

The young poet he talked to kept coming back to the virgin in his litanies of debasement
yet when he mentioned it the boy at first seemed confused. "Oh, you mean Mary," he said

12.9.12

Tree brought into the room
then bound in strands of light

12.10.12

made up
my mind

12.11.12

It was wrong to tell the girl
that nothing can be known.

12.12.12

wrote *à la rose des douzes,* granddaughter whose
birthday this is and will never be so again

12.13.12

out of a day that began half-mad madly crafted something akin to normalcy
like that Swede who painted a facsimile for his driver's license photograph

12.14.12

The slaughter of the innocents
is marked upon our foreheads

12.15.12

Six around the table they sat
Pesach out of season this year

12.16.12

Charlotte, Daniel, Olivia, Josephine, Ana, Dylan, Madeline, Catherine, Chase, Jesse, James, Grace, Emilie, Jack, Noah, Caroline, Jessica, Benjamin, Avielle, Allison

12.17.12

Twenty four hours of rain, more or less, heading toward the winter solstice
or the end of baktun 13, what happens next, too, more or less in question

12.18.12

This month more than any here so far consumed by meditations on number,
although when I count the entries to date they amount to a little less than half

12.19.12

Bodhisattva of the hot dog counter
finds samādhi in the dentist's chair

12.20.12

hiss of the scissors through gilt paper
falling ribbon whispers to the table

12.21.12

Sinatra carols from the room below
outside cars depart a holiday party

12.22.12

dead
tome

12.23.12

An unseasonable desire for desire quells itself
as meanwhile winter's first gusts slowly desist

12.24.12

We have come to the age where
the carols outnumber our lessons

12.25.12

She tends to the flames throughout the eve, twenty-four candles,
six oil lamps, four Swedish änglaspel, the numbers not significant

12.26.12

Mid-storm along the icy road down to the river in the grotesque carnival of emergency lights
two mangled cars glow in the ditch like a carnal couple entwined in motley postcoital sheets

12.27.12

Under the confectionary snow a shelf of grisaille
soiled slush flowing black as captured night

12.28.12

We hang the feeder, fill it with black-oil sunflower seed, and go back in;
okay, she says (standing by the window) where are the birds?

12.29.12

axle broke, snow before noon,
thirteenth moon starts to wane

12.30.12

after his three decade ago fall *c'est toujours la veille
d'après-demain*, the eve of the day after tomorrow

12.31.12

the boy who long ago showed my father razor clams and starfish
scrambled nearby stone jetties after his death, asking are you sad?

1.1.13

quietly we keep company late into this first day,
festivities displaced, our guests come and gone

1.2.13

Green dignity of the tree
at the last naked before us

1.3.13

Two days before leaving and with nothing left but to wait
an odd sense of freedom comes as if a glimpse of dying

1.4.13

To celebrate her birth a diadem of greenhouse vegetables is laid before her on single pins:
slim, bearded carrot, sweet celery stalk, bright virginal lettuce, thin radish, radiant chou-fleur.

1.5.13

The shoulder of the crusted snowbank along the drive resists the New Year's melt
as we hold each other in the silence and fading sun of this post-solstice mid-afternoon

1.6.13

The poem so carefully composed at her side before dawn slipped from my mind.
So, too, will I slip away before long, yet she and the dawn and lost poem remain.

1.7.13

Awoke *trois fois* during the course of a single *journée*, first to the clamor of the morning airplane,
then *le cascade des écolieres dans le jardin Villemin, enfin dans la Voie lactée* of jetlagged night

1.8.13

A dream of herbal sea wrack arrayed like tattered lace
and the time she lifted imaginary skirts, laughing at herself

1.9.13

Never enough light *dans La Ville-Lumière*
lugging home an armful from BHV

1.10.13

As the night descends these ancient beams groan with memories of wounded hearts
of Franciscans, soldiers and *des anges des Récollets* and now three Kurdish martyrs

1.11.13

Dispatches of the death vigil for the Finnish poet arrive by email
I remember his great farmer's hands like his countryman the cellist

1.12.13

La chamane kenyane laughing over mint tea in a tapas bar, Canal Saint Martin,
Buddhist nun's closecropped hair above dancing eyes and amaranth knit jilbab

1.13.13

Grésil glacial slantwise along rue des Récollets
distracts an absent-minded seeker into the wrong cafe

1.14.13

Soft snow lies upon the lawns of *le jardin*
empty at this hour, bare boughs swaying

1.15.13

Goes out *sous le soleil*, comes back *sous la grisaille*
 you and *les deux* day to day *s'enverser en janvier*

1.16.13

wake without the network remembering
her saying you don't like not to be connected

1.17.13

Wednesday night at le Bougnat *tout le monde* sings along to Brassens'
song of being nestled neath an umbrella against a slice of paradise

1.18.13

Quelque chose à faire, something to do
Out in the snow to see Didi and GoGo

1.19.13

At Celeste Gourmand garlic shoots, spicy cabbage, dumplings, and—*à deux reprises*—
fried noodles are followed by chicken, beef, fish, and tofu, *chaque avec leurs piments*

1.20.13

Coquettish on the sofa she in video chat
enfolds my midnight into her early evening

1.21.13

Four ruffles and flourishes come
to one *un monde à part et enneigé*

1.22.13

These lines written in clear liquid
an eremite's regime in a convent aerie

1.23.13

A single boiled egg seems a world sometimes
below a sole cloud torn from moldy bread

1.24.13

who he was four days ago
hungrily shows himself

1.25.13

in her rhinestone fez she crawls into her mother's bed
feeding her sips from a baby's cup as she mewls

1.26.13

having none of my advantages save the cold, still my brother monks settled themselves
amidst visions not much different I suppose from my *fantasmes télévisuels sous-titrés*

1.27.13

out through the Roman gate on Saint-Martin and cross at Pont au Change
back to the Bastille sur le Pont de Sully chanting *homos, hétéros, tous égaux*

1.28.13

cent brouillons dans mon lit
"how it's supposed to be," I guess

1.29.13

warm southwesterly
sways winter trees

1.30.13

I realize that I do not speak
the language that I think

1.31.13

the fourth magi wanders off before the unveiling and all that entails
the desert night familiar and the dromedary thud muffled by the sand

2.1.13

tired of this bliss
called emptiness

2.2.13

Contractions of time offset by the intimacy of elongations
our lives become a lesson in social space writ in thin rain

2.3.13

I brought my black suit to Paris thinking to attend the mayor's reception
but when the four a.m phone call came I began to think more darkly

2.4.13

the swollen waters of the canal seem to levitate at dusk
miroirs en cuivre floating there beyond the cobble path

2.5.13

L'ascenseur en panne again
four flights up to *la vie bohême*

2.6.13

tandis que je traque mon frère puîné, a lash of wind and rain
agite le couvent ancien at midnight as I toss restless in my bed

2.7.13

le ruban de l'aube of tangerine grosgrain
flares and disappears before the gaining grey

2.8.13

the day removed from itself
like a hidden card

2.9.13

Bonjour cher voisin says the la Montréalaise, a literalist
Bonjour chère voisine, I reply. *Alors que la bonne? Elle rit*

2.10.13

carneval and *le nouvel an chinois* converge
in drums and dragons and horizontal snow

2.11.13

the plain, pretty physicist makes her way
among *normaliens* to where the poet waits

2.12.13

mardi gras of thin Thai soup,
pizza, and a Danish policier

2.13.13

red apples suspended in a blue plastic sack
from a window above a vitrine of fetish art

2.14.13

Two old cavaliers and a young new divorcée slurp oysters and sip Graves
then nibble white chocolate hearts *chacun avec leur couverture rouge.*

2.15.13

amid the white roses and clematis and *vingtaine d'iris cachés*
Tom des Fleurs tucks woody stalks of rosemary in bloom

2.16.13

For dessert he sets out two tranches from a round of *chevre de Solange*
beside the gleaming bloody purple segments of the Moro oranges

2.17.13

wake twice in a fright from a dream of being
unable to awake from these same dreams

2.18.13

She writes: "Really sad—he is so sick. He gave us the thumbs up a few times.
Made a fist (sign of strength) when we told him we believed he'd get better."

2.19.13

after a *demi* of rouge
the lights of the canal

2.20.13

no story here
nor here none

2.21.13

all day anticipating
the Phoenician city

2.22.13

from the window of the TGV between Arles and Aix
suddenly recognize the color of Cezanne's *marne rouge*

2.23.13

Along a high path above *les falaises de calcaire*
the Mediterranean sings its *chant venteuse et spumeux*

2.24.13

Takes a tumble under a full moon,
sea and the Mistral and black dog howling

2.25.13

It is farther by far to return
here from where you've been

2.26.13

she kneels at the head of the supine guitar
then slowly runs long palms along its length

2.27.13

I cannot let myself— or simply cannot— feel these things,
yet the sharks are there and glide unseen beneath the ice.

2.28.13

here where there hides
the silence of my soul

3.1.13

how tired the priest becomes
of the dry host, the empty paten

3.2.13

dinner alone the
theater the train

3.3.13

along the loggia at the *Chapelle expiatoire*
two dark, pretty whores chat under an arch

3.4.13

les élèves en vacances
le printemps est annoncé

3.5.13

caught up in the smell of perfume and the feeling of peace as the people press forward
toward the altar of the virgin after the young nun song leader extinguishes the candles

3.6.13

tolled
told

3.7.13

Below the still point of the rivet on the engine cowl a low sun
gilds the tufted paths the wind carves in the clouds that cover the Atlantic

3.8.13

I keep seeing him, not dead more than forty-eight hours,
There is so much to do, he says, and everyone is so nice.

3.9.13

The guest of honor will not arrive
But sleeps alone in the empty parlor

3.10.13

By the third night of waking everyone sits exhausted,
cakes going dry on the platters, cups of wine unfinished

3.11.13

oak boat fitted out she kisses
his cold brow, *iníon a athair go deo*

3.12.13

Everyone gone *chez eux*:
the living and the dead.

3.13.13

"Tu renaîtras à nouveau, oui, renaîtras à nouveau, ma poussière, après un bref repos"
and the emails keep coming with these snippets, swathes, choruses, covering you with garlands

3.14.13

Settled into the business of it, he counts
imaginary jars upon an empty shelf

3.15.13

Idus Martiae consolantur, or so Cicero wrote, although for my own consolation I sought
my brother's iTunes playlist and his interview about Catullus' poem on the death of his brother

3.16.13

posts the elegy to London
definition of a gratuitous act

3.17.13

The accumulated grief in the postings on his Facebook wall adds up to nothing:
They wish him to rest in peace, heaven has a new angel, they will never forget.

3.18.13

out of control downhill on the icy road toward the river
trees like faceless ghosts and she calls his name aloud

3.19.13

versions of the sad songs
and still the night goes on

3.20.13

equi/nox

3.21.13

Spring arrives under a blanket of days old snow, rattle of a pick-up
loading outside at 6:00 a.m. arousing the sleepers into uncertain embrace

3.22.13

Along the farm road specters of my mother and brother as much there in the diesel fume and dust
as in the trunk of the sacred oak in whose embrace once she kept her promise to tell me of paradise

3.23.13

over dinner we trade stories of the blessed virgin
and having seen our own mothers after their deaths

3.24.13

My soul a mercury bead suspended along avenues
spoking outward across the city I walked for hours.

3.25.13

partnerless three female cardinals peck among the scree of dull black hulls and seeds
below the feeder on this grey afternoon at the edge of spring as the storm skirts overhead

3.26.13

green exhalation in ascent
under the yellowed timothy

3.27.13

three weeks now you
persist in being dead

3.28.13

Puppet show in a waste-strewn field at the edge of the city where
owls, puffins, and grebes flap and preen like wind-blown plastic sacks

3.29.13

On Good Friday we talk of chord changes
common time gone to irrational meters

3.30.13

Nearly four months to the day, sitting where we last saw him
we sing half-forgotten lyrics of breaking through to somewhere

3.31.13

gnosis in New Jersey
the stone rolled back

4.1.13

The widow sees her husband in a dream,
his back a mappemunde, each mark known to her

4.2.13

he has made it possible to conceive of
what comes after sleep no longer comes

4.3.13

The void between far fences
this shadow marked in crossing

4.4.13

A month by weeks less
two days by calendar

4.5.13

 "Window open on spring air
workmen below float zydeco." (CG)

4.6.13

suburban concerns of a Saturday morning
now compounding to include the logistics of loss

4.7.13

early morning tracery upon their bodies
how Neith reweaves the world daily

4.8.13

weeping westward at intervals (to a Beatles soundtrack)
first paralleling the retracted river bed then the long lake plain

4.9.13

blanket of grave backfill studded with marble shards and what look to be sheared masonry brick
the mound strewn with bleach-yellow desiccated flowers and reddish marl that crumbles to the touch

4.10.13

Thirty years after she left us I move through the rooms of the house of the son who has joined her
even so calling his name above the rain and thunder, at first a shout and then softly as a brother

4.11.13

The birds below the feeder scatter before
the shadow of the figure in the high window

4.12.13

awaited a
way to say

4.13.13

caught in a feeling of (or for) leaden
form having outlived the letting go

4.14.13

Dreams of units of measure that— jar, the grave, depleted coil of coaxial cable,
choree, couplet, sleep and dream themselves—it takes no priestess to decipher

4.15.13

beneath the gaudy riffle of the wetland cascade a whisper
where the old course still tucks among half-mossed rocks

4.16.13

here is what we have been thinking
there is another place not far away

4.17.13

I seek out my brother in the shadows
and ask has he seen me anywhere

4.18.13

To surprise oneself
a sly kind of suicide

4.19.13

shot through with the tiresome murk of what the ancients named melancholy
or how the tree man glossed the chemistry of the black walnut as he coiled his ropes

4.20.13

 "saying things in time" (Creeley) where the phrase is doubled, i.e., the melodiousness we
used to call prosody but lately have taken to calling sonics, and, of course, seasonable reply

4.21.13

chalked lines scrubbed from the pavement for a week less in denial than disavowal
until finally the monster of our own making is found cowering in the bloody prow

4.22.13

The dreams come back like winter birds
exiled beyond the horizon until now.

4.23.13

waits
word

4.24.13

Persistent rumble of what is not thunder, fireworks she says,
unseasonably and impractical; he suggests artillery perhaps

4.25.13

narcissus: papyraceus, poeticus, jonquilla candolle,
daffodil, asphodel, affodell, daffadown dilly, amen

4.26.13

By way of representing an image of order to the world he commends
coincidence of the spring moth's wing and milkweed floss held lazily aloft

4.27.13

what went on this morning or after
noon or this evening until now lost

4.28.13

the specter's shy smile in the kitchen an apparition of Freud's "*es spukt*"
there's no sense, he says, talking about what nothing can be done about

4.29.13

end of nothing palpable
month no sack of spelt

4.30.13

magnolia in petal fall
skirt demurely at her feet

5.1.13

Patsy Cline on the car radio sings "Time for me will be no more,"
empty small town streets unwinding in the blank of noon beyond.

5.2.13

tried every trick
but to tell the truth

5.3.13

Softly she declares a shift in the "forming color" of these hills,
the indigo gone to rose-tipped chartreuse this wanton spring

5.4.13

"We saw dolphins in the Potomac the earliest ever," says one waterman to another at Courtney's,
as he settles into a beer, a coke for his lady, a dozen blue crabs, and a basket of fries and rockfish

5.5.13

Whitecaps lap the causeway beneath overcast just beyond
the unmarked barbed wire fence of the not so secret drone base

5.6.13

this a περίπλους
now and then

5.7.13

They come as birds, the dead, and so signal themselves
sans language or expression, save their soaring and sung presence

5.8.13

a.m.coffee *avec une fille bilingue* she drinking tea, lumpia lunch with a young poet in a long skirt,
followed by a supper of hay-colored *paillards de veau* cooked in turmeric tinted ghee for my love

5.9.13

Left space for what I have not done
as if it were the mark of something

5.10.13

 "O eyes that loke" Olson's pidgin epigraph inverted now
in the cry of this fahter recalling his first sone's first morning

5.11.13

Side by side on the train we trade emailed accounts of dreams of the lost,
passing the phone from hand to hand, touching the screen to revive it.

5.12.13

Progress here would be measured how?
Say, having come this far circling back again.

5.13.13

in the middle of a series of three eclipses
feelings of loss are reported to be universal

5.14.13

I watch men at work all day.
This watching thought my work.

5.15.13

mindful again of the cascade of *this* and *says* and *here*
the neutering of actual things, of what really was said where

5.16.13

thrice woven into the *drôlerie* of "creamed corn consommé," C sees
her monogram, *comme un petit chemin* through alphabetic byways

5.17.13

as if astronauts the contractors maneuver Silverados to opposite lanes and dock
thence through the truck windows offer bleak disputations of all they survey

5.18.13

consider ryegrass and fescue in a solitary blue carton of recycled cardboard on a narrow shelf
against rabbit two ways, pickled ramps, and a hash of wild mushrooms set out on a china plate

5.19.13

This rainy Sunday afternoon becomes a ceremony of elements
scrubbing clay from three ragged stones arranged at the garden edge

5.20.13

giddy after a bottle of chenin blanc
we plant clematis at twilight

5.21.13

freshening breeze off the river after sunset
haze-wreathed crescent moon waning

5.22.13

thought myself
here last night

5.23.13

waiting for a letter from someone
who does not know to write me

5.24.13

in a stupor on the sofa
delirious dreams of rain

5.25.13

the river swollen brown after two days of showers
white caps roll shoreward, allium bending in the wind

5.26.13

sun to shadow to sun he circles
searching the one who knows him

5.27.13

For some time the sequence of days yields an obvious, even wearisome, narrative
making it hard to pick out our hero as the shadow slipping through the penumbra

5.28.13

westward in the way such things are done now
then back in three days, and so never really gone

5.29.13

Tracking the sunset high above the high desert over rippled clouds and grey chasms at dusk
the light nonetheless receding, misted landscape folding into itself like segments of a paper fan

5.30.13

In the shade of the portal of the dry Santa Fe *corte* tanagers feed on oranges
among the young poplars as the assembled grandparents talk of the graduate

5.31.13

The first day of the Tres Lagunas fire the sun hung suspended at twilight,
a perfect vermillion disk in a marigold haze above the line of violet

6.1.13

Just beyond Cochiti pueblo along I-25 at midday he spies a ghostly Kopishtaya
moving silently in her high ash-white moccasins down through a dry arroyo

6.2.13

in the dream she was following her father's blue car his daughter says on the telephone
but she can't remember whether once she caught up with him she told him he was dead

6.3.13

constant trill of temple bells
cicadas across the river

6.4.13

seers on the radio on successive days proffer what wisdom they can:
life's good although to be happy you've got to control bad thoughts

6.5.13

A monk's work but not his temperament
I sweep sand over stones, sweep sand again

6.6.13

A quarter of this newly inaugurated year within a year now gone
with him, there in stop-time, poet on Youtube waving goodbye

6.7.13

adolescence onward every leave-taking a reckoning
how they used to gather in the front hallway as I left

6.8.13

The bride still in her gown smokes cigarettes among her maids
beneath the carport of the airport Best Western past midnight

6.9.13

Empty morning after the boys' school 50th reunion
empty bed, empty airport, empty seat beside me

6.10.13

all day only spoke face-to-face with two women, each smiling, both Asian, both
softly asking questions, after that the telephone and then the fact of constant rain

6.11.13

thatch of moss latching on
where the stone sheared

6.12.13

flash on their faces along the Seine at night in the photograph forms masks of the three graces
"from whose eyes as they glanced flowed love that unnerves the limbs," or so says Hesiod

6.13.13

we walk in separate cities
rain falling there and here

6.14.13

when the interviewers come back into the room he finds himself now someone else
on a new shore in a new house casting a shadow he's only seen before in a dream

6.15.13

Out upon the Red Hook pier at midnight under a ripe quarter moon
La Liberté looming across the lower bay, tug and a dark barge passing

6.16.13

into the stillness
of these words

6.17.13

Tango by txt
Orly to NYC

6.18.13

The drum major's bowlegged daughter
fashions herself here out of whole cloth

6.19.13

How closely do you think you have approached
any serious understanding of what you do here?

6.20.13

In the shade of the honeysuckle allée small rabbits zig-zag away and tuck beneath the fence
while on the ridge just beyond crows gorge on cicadas, their gold wings glittering as they fall

6.21.13

the birds and we awake and know this longest day is but a mark the gnomon makes upon this disk
the nodus of a passing second upon a declination line which once traversed no creature lives to tell

6.22.13

Perigee full moon trails the solstice by a day as Magicicada Brood II wanes;
in the heat of afternoon I combed stones from where the grass will not grow.

6.23.13

He looks to where she
thinks she sees him here

6.24.13

the road at the ecological station is already baking at ten a.m. as his ghost lolls in and out of focus
leaning against the ancient trunk at the center of the shade circle made by the limbs of the Druid oak

6.25.13

A second morning he shows himself as a worm, maroon and moist on the tamped white gravel
the Buddhist and the boy in me contending until I recognize him wriggling ahead on the path

6.26.13

Makes the extravagant gesture, a flight to Paris for a three day stay four months hence for instance,
not as if death could be held off or the line re-reeled, but because to act bears its burden lightly.

6.27.13

gray gouache of soft fog erases all but the curve of the opposite shore
a frail form afloat upon a wedge of silver shimmer just above the river

6.28.13

month lurching to its end in steam and sullen sun
already damp with exhaustion, blank weeks ahead

6.29.13

The cicadas are gone where they have always been
here with us who will not live to hear them again

6.30.13

Keying in "Find" then "Find again":
Now fifteen instances of lost.

7.1.13

With her Dutch girl hair and bow and belted frock and patent leather Mary Janes,
the girl in the photograph who my mother became would have passed ninety today.

7.2.13

old pain in a new form
seeker back from a journey

7.3.13

when I bring her the stalk she tells me again of the hollyhock dolls of her girlhood
how they'd pluck the stigma and put it as a head above the skirt then make them dance

7.4.13

The dull cannonade comes at dusk as towns up and down the river salute one another,
peony shells followed by chrysanthemum and crossettes while fireflies rise in silence.

7.5.13

after the apparition, vertigo
the matador vomits in the sun

7.6.13

along the line between what happens to him and what at end he alone mutely will have done
he discerns in a shadow beside him the hidden face of the self whose name he will never know

7.7.13

In the morning she prays to the sun god and then the chants for protection, destruction, and creation;
later at the temple she invokes the god of energy, of Ganesha, of beginnings, asking for compassion.

7.8.13

we number the days of the heat
each day starting over with one

7.9.13

If the week becomes a path of rough stone
here is the jagged place I began to stumble

7.10.13

West coast day game already played by the time he sends the text
that you only read after he has called. And do you recall this pain?

7.11.13

Sipping hay-colored Umbrian Grechetto Bianco from a black bottle at the fish house as she explains
how our two kinds of fried flounder "like lemon or grey sole or fluke are all more or less the same"

7.12.13

In sullen frustration
hear her breathing

7.13.13

The Charles pools into a circle cul de sac at the end of a narrow slip
where teenage couples on mall dates chew burgers from greasy wrappers

7.14.13

Brunch with the Romanian sisters and their dark-haired sons in Cambridge
reminiscing upon *le Quatorze Juillet l'année dernière* along the beach at Royan

7.15.13

The old woman recites her mad litany as they strap her onto the gurney:
"Bi-polar, blue eyes, no friends, river water, slim men, girl in a uniform."

7.16.13

In from the blasting heat of Park Avenue to cool before the countenance of Shakyamuni,
serenely sculpted from softly polished schist the Buddha makes the earth touching gesture

7.17.13

we sit at the insula of their Cobble Hill kitchen table as my son explains
how the mirror neurons link the old and new brains into care for others

7.18.13

my neck a plinth for nearly seventy years
wearies of the foolish weight it bears up

7.19.13

after twice seventy-eight miles of traffic in hundred degree heat
the air conditioner in the old hotel rumbles and groans all night

7.20.13

gin and tonic after Vicodin
ice pack after hot compress

7.21.13

tide slides lower beneath
a somnolent melon moon

7.22.13

morning glory on the shoulder of day lily
heat wave lapsing for now into memory

7.23.13

The night heron that settles standing in the muck shallows of the bay at White's
presides over a sleepy congregation of mud-drab ducks, all of them gone at dawn

7.24.13

white sails of a lone sloop along an upwind reach,
weather coming around with it, sky and river pewter

7.25.13

Bluegrass fiddle starting up as I cross where Wappinger's Estuary meets the river,
older than me now in death my brother asks "Shouldn't this music make you happy?"

7.26.13

Traveling marimba troupe in Washington Square
thrums a Shona prayer "for those who've felt a loss"

7.27.13

This fool's sacred resolve to let everything go
only gives to the future what it already holds

7.28.13

On the day of departure awoke weary
already having traveled half the night

7.29.13

"No point in weeping over Beethoven's grave," says the woman at Grogan's pub
to the callow young man who has just described his plans to do so on his holiday

7.30.13

At Leenane she looks back to where they nestle along the fjord and pronounces
"Here surely the clouds and the mountains are always a part of each other."

7.31.13

Framed by the parlour window at Currevagh House
six small islands head out like a flotilla on Lough Corrib

8.1.13

From a putty-colored dimly lit B&B looking out on a dog house
we walk down to Westport quay and gaze upon the distant Reek

8.2.13

Not far from the austere desmesne where Aillil Finn once reigned over Gleann Néifinne
the boy, my father's father's father, left this farm for the coal hills of Pennsylvania

8.3.13

Nephin shows its skewbald flank as we come along the road from Boghadoon,
ducking behind a veil of mist at Glenavenue before cupping the sun in its wells.

8.4.13

Outside the pubs near Croke Park at dusk the Mayo men smoke and preen in green and red,
their beures beside them right tarted-up in pink GAA kits and neon pink platform sneakers.

8.5.13

Out from the canal in Portobello twilight along South Richmond Street up toward Iveagh Gardens
setting forth in the footsteps of my other ancestral line, the one born of imagination and exile

8.6.13

Like us having come back to the same thing, thirteen ducks
dawn and dusk squat on the same two logs in the shallows

8.7.13

looking where
we came from

8.8.13

Two magic girls: one a wanderer who bade me read of Morgaine, her son, and the isle of apples;
the other, my then young cousin, who sang of "partridge, pheasant, hare and duck" 'neath Nephin.

8.9.13

The wine he "quaffs" has a nose of rose petals and agony
or so the brother of the counselor jests at his wedding supper

8.10.13

We sit in the shade at a plastic table set among gravel and weeds by the shore of an ordinary lake
and the girl who brings us Chilean Sauvignon Blanc in a plastic bucket tells us we look so romantic

8.11.13

make our way like pack animals up switchbacks from Black Creek but then lose track of the trail,
the second time this summer we turn back having failed to view the river from Pitch Pine Overlook

8.12.13

thinking he forgot the Buddha
brings to mind this poem

8.13.13

The ex and current wives stand together in agreement
that the young wife doesn't know yet not to chill tomatoes

8.14.13

To what end precisely do I make my circuit between these weedy margins
alive with chicory and mustard along the road paralleling the swollen river

8.15.13

veering toward midnight
wordlessly in no wise

8.16.13

the quiet of the gravid tunnel from which no wayfarer returns
nor any cry emerges to those who await their time to pass

8.17.13

Through the lens of this ground glass nodule I see myself
in such calm as attends a man alone at the end of a train platform

8.18.13

Nearing Mt Sinai Harbor along the shore road fastidious swans
feed at dusk, gobs of black muck drooping from their yellow bills

8.19.13

Just before Monday dawn the fear shows its stark, indifferent face
like the opacity that spawns it a mix of solid elements and lucencies

8.20.13

only the hovering blue moon
without apprehension this night

8.21.13

the river gently filling in slow, estuarine increase, mist lingering
in tatters on the ridges and small bays, in sympathy with my fears

8.22.13

This last morning, this first morning, the sun, hazy and engorged
dawns again above a ledge of grey clouds low along the horizon

8.23.13

The reprieve the physician can give grants no longer than its utterance
yet Elisheba and Zechariah shuffle out exulting in temporary resurrection

8.24.13

morning's brightness ever now
imbued with twilight's hues

8.25.13

The girl prodigy's account depicts Paris as monochromic,
a cobble of calcareous rubble like a beach below Sacré-Cœur

8.26.13

Mindful of Berryman's injunction about fame and a letter from a young man,
which when we were young men my poet friend John and I read to each other.

8.27.13

 "It's not so much a cloud of unknowing as unknowing in broad daylight," the poet, Wladek, writes
speaking both of and through fathers and how we grow old together like and unlike them alike

8.28.13

Amber lamps of the tug glide downriver in the night,
bright circus wagon pulled by groaning black steeds.

8.29.13

lone crow flies under a low sky
up Division Street to Point

8.30.13

freshening breeze up from the river in an exhausted rush
as a world away the bard of Mossbawn draws his last breath

8.31.13

At Lovers Leap the two of them turn back well before the iron bridge
that leads to the ledge from which Lillinonah and her paramour plunged.

9.1.13

a year ago a like mood
descended rain too then

9.2.13

languorous in her long green dress at dusk
Metope shepherds her daughters riverward

9.3.13

"The world owes me nothing," Ryokan's dunce exults in the poem my brother emails,
 dunce to dunce at dawn, after Milarepa becomes "too much about sorcery for [his] heart."

9.4.13

then waiting for
not waiting again

9.5.13

come humble to the table
master of nothing

9.6.13

a half year after ambushed again, him dying
like that, before I could swim out to save him

9.7.713

Sloop coming around runs upriver with the wind
blue hull through sun-dapple and green cat's paw

9.8.13

She is angry that, on that far coast where she has been just once, the world
does not work as she understands it and is unfriendly because she drives a car

9.9.13

Lingers at the table reluctant to go
back to the life she is left defending

9.10.13

his son will become
a father he tells him

9.11.13

all morning in a frenzy over space in the hold
his place the old obsession of the eldest son

9.12.13

The five geese flying up from the river in a chevron
going nowhere yet rehearse ancient patterns of return.

9.13.13

your heartbeat in this first sonogram molto presto, little one,
say Bach's Sonata in G minor played by Vermeer's luitspelster

9.14.13

on a perfect autumn day in the city on the sidewalk outside the folklore museum comes the news
that death's shadow once again has interposed itself upon the cusp of atonement and renewal

9.15.13

Far from Dark Town "exciting events" still show themselves hereabouts
two women demurely squatting in long skirts balance upon high heels

9.16.13

The exigencies of plumbing play their part
and mark the ceiling in these chronicles.

9.17.13

Through the arbor of the Shakespeare Garden on a golden afternoon
delights in finding her finding him coming toward her unbeknownst

9.18.13

From the river's radiant surface lifts an airy fabric of silk, languorous smoke,
and cotton filaments drifting toward an unseen bank before the sun's advancing

9.19.13

only late in his life does the lion discover
this prowling is what purpose he's allowed

9.20.13

if memory is prayer he wonders
what it is not to remember to pray

9.21.13

Baritone chimes clang in the shifting wind
on the eve of the autumnal equinox

9.22.13

her gaze the salt that fixes his
imago upon the copper plate

9.23.13

blue post-it note pledging "neverending love"
fastened by chance upon an empty Viagra vial

9.24.13

stumbling in quickstep
toward an inevitable ascent

9.25.13

The day bracketed by cellphone photographs of the sky mirrored on the water:
its morning surface dun furled with gossamer mist, at dusk plum mottled pink.

9.26.13

I force myself from a dream of the descent no one awakes from,
a drowning man cresting above a numbing sea, no shore in sight

9.27.13

They sit across the table sharing crab and corn fritters and then chocolate cake
her poems on a folded sheet in his pocket, his on the screen she holds in her lap

9.28.13

says she feels she's missing
something she cannot name

9.29.13

Sunday spent inside the house
an inadvertent hermitage

9.30.13

Waving gaily on barren stalks two vaguely whorish
hollyhocks lean toward the road twirling red skirts

10.1.13

unable to discern the etiology of the distress within him
the would-be pilgrim nonetheless ingests pills and potions

10.2.13

a movement neither
leaving nor setting forth

10.3.13

In the thin light of dawn the black slabs of the Warsaw skyline
rise above a yellowed smog like a rotogravure graveyard

10.4.13

On Grażyny Street in Kraków Mariusz says had you come
years ago you might have passed Milosz or Symborska here

10.5.13

There in the room where he wrote his poems and died on a morning not unlike this
we look down on człowiek noblitsa's garden and pass his Waterman pen among us.

10.6.13

Unraveling westward the gray skein of this endless five p.m.,
which when we reach it will leave us looking back on nothing

10.7.13

The haunted young man finds his solace in plotting mathematical topologies,
cyclic and periodic trajectories he traces upon the ruled paper of his notebook.

10.8.13

one
self

10.9.13

You show yourself today for who you are, little one, faery trace of silver
sounding head and heart and spine outlined there upon a darkened screen

10.10.13

Attacks the black walnuts with military precision
laying stripes of dark mulch behind the machine

10.11.13

The fact that no one told him how to live
left him to figure out how to die by himself

10.12.13

Widowed now more than half a year each day she wakes
thinking surely he will come back from vacation soon

10.13.13

To have mixed her mother's ashes with the earth
seems an odd concept the childless daughter says

10.14.13

Between the oak leaf and the marble tile he rests
two seasons passed, unmarked grave compassed green

10.15.13

We deal out our time together by hours
gray, cafe, landmark, porch, bistro, auto

10.16.13

Having undertaken what someone called an archeology of grief there seems little left
but to wait out the rainy morning listening to Berlioz alone in this nondescript motel

10.17.13

West from the cafe terrace along le bassin de la Villette toward Stalingrad
a wedge of afternoon sun lingers under the boil of grey clouds just come in

10.18.13

Trod the cobble towpath along the canal this morning and looked for him where he left me then sat watching the bateau Arletty lower in the locks before the dark vault of the Bastille

10.19.13

L'été de Saint-Michel having given way to l'été de Saint-Martin, the full moon slips unseen into penumbral eclipse under which American children toss oak leaves in the Luxembourg garden

10.20.13

Ce que est une ville
c'est ses souvenirs

What a city is
is its memories

10.21.13

Ce déjeuner takes place not *sur l'herbes* but *entre la cascade* and the jackhammers *dans des Buttes Chaumont* this his first birthday *apres il a passé de vie à trépas*

10.22.13

"I was in our back garden, in sunlight, among flowers, when the call came," Heaney writes, and the sentence can be no more clear to any of us who, like him, have received such news.

10.23.13

Beyond the last remaining dock the void,
the fog from and of and into which I walk

10.24.13

Today the river tide-swollen
crows picking at road carrion

10.25.13

In the dream I walked knowingly past my father as he sat along some European shore
but woke before recalling he's long been dead, living only two years more than I am now

10.26.13

along the old mountain carriageway in the lulling emptiness of a late October Saturday
copper oaks and maples of burnt sienna flare in the midst of an otherwise drab panorama.

10.27.13

what it is he walks away from
perhaps is why he cannot say

10.28.13

steel gray chop
just after dawn

10.29.13

The circling geese try then fail to form a V then move on in desultory
 asymmetry, haphazard squadron forming a jagged grin above the river

10.30.13

In the grosgrain hour that binds the fraying night to dawn
the bay emptied of its docks lies calm beneath an inky voile

10.31.1

Dawn an amethyst haze over river and hills out of which it's surely his joking voice that calls this
the national holiday of the dead, yet whose voice then goes on to speak of heaven I cannot discern

11.1.13

Having come in from the wind and rain at Stop & Shop the meager pile in Mawmaw's cart contains
2 single-cup servings of bright mixed fruit and a pack of 10 wrapped slices of pale yellow cheese

11.2.13

Outside Pine Plains sunset's narrowing ray path
garlands the Berkshire foothills with a gilt corona

11.3.13

Fall's extra hour spent
without ever going out

11.4.13

Little one twists and turns for her twenty-week pictures
principessa nell'utero covering her face with her hands

11.5.13

he doesn't think he wants
to die now in his sleep

11.6.13

The procession of low rust-colored hills along this familiar track an augury:
though autumn mayhap have gilded, once flaring it will before long anneal.

11.7.13

Crossing at Broadway and 42nd in Times Square I meet the Buddha's gaze and nod,
he fixes his eyes upon me and makes the Pran Mudra sign which I return in kind.

11.8.13

wood smoke and chimes mix in the north-blown wind,
river traced with lace, leaf scent of low tide receding

11.9.13

This body born to him so long ago he thinks become a tramp steamer,
which in some port town he'll walk away from, watching as it sails on

11.10.13

at noon a dark hem of rainy gusts descends in a sudden in Port Jefferson where
we walked the dappled tatter of mild autumn along the town trail an hour earlier

11.11.13

Six narrow keystones of interstitial light rib the gravel in parallel
where the shrouded boats sit perpendicular to the dawn at White's

11.12.13

a curtain of dull snow falls from ashen clouds
melting to a snakeskin pattern on the pavement

11.13.13

The great blue heron takes refuge on a low bough
hunched from the chill like a Capuchin at matins

11.14.13

His face frozen into a grin before the swelling tide, the swelling wind,
he watches her taillights slowly disappear along the rise beyond town

11.15.13

I conclude that my grief consists in this
absence of belief in my own real presence

11.16.13

At winter's edge a thin wind rustles within
empty chambers of the paper wasp nest.

11.17.13

another Sabbath without having left the house
caught up in my own scripture, acolyte to myself

11.18.13

After the rain the lane to Rabbit Island is strewn with pale pointed leaves,
a pell-mell school of silver river herring that swim among yellow moths.

11.19.13

sunrise stamps a precise yellow-gold belt upon the far bank
between a gunmetal chemise of cloud and the river's plum skirt

11.20.13

He thinks himself become more and more lizard-like
skin crusted, eyes hooded, locomotion archosaurian

11.21.13

pale swirl of icy exhalation
the river yellowed ivory

11.22.13

crossing Cazenovia Park alone in unseasonable mist this day fifty years ago the news new in my ears
raster images of the slain young king and the queen's blood-stained suit indelibly etched our horizon

11.23.13

abed relatively late cold sunny Saturday
now he lingers here afterward exactly

11.24.13

Opening an eight-year-old Russian River pinot two years before the cellar notes recommend
a dread thought comes as I realize I may be gone before this year's vintage is ready to drink

11.25.13

a skim of first ice in the cove along River Street
where the circling geese were wont to shelter

11.26.13

The nor'easter here dissolves into rain on rain
lines between lanes lost beneath a black mirror

11.27.13

This chronicle of an old fool
doesn't even interest himself

11.28.13

They sit around the long table like a shipwrecked company
thinking still of the raft and the long nights on a dark sea

11.29.13

I go down alone to the tumult of the motel breakfast room
the sole non-celebrant the whole of this long weekend

11.30.13

leaving where I have not been
back to where I have not gone

12.01.13

circle forth
and back

12.02.13

His death to him like a clock in the night
indecipherable glow not to be counted on

12.03.13

dreams that he could make a hut of fog
escaping their dreary accounting there

12.04.13

They erect the inverted tent of the portacrib in the center of the living room for practice
and well before her apparition the mystery of her shines forth from its fulgent confine

12.05.13

Of four paths one ends in nothing, another in undifferentiated energy,
the third another's track of sorrows, the fourth an incalculable paradise

12.06.13

The young poet accounts his hour and a half discussion with a young woman of his acquaintance,
anent attitude as a philosophical concept, re: Stockhausen's Licht, of Lucifer, and the twin towers

12.07.13

Over the network a woman says the wind is blowing off the Baltic just as darkness falls in Paris
while in Atlanta the actress, a physician, gasps despite herself when he utters the word orgasmic

12.08.13

a week to the day after the derailment at Spuyten Duyvil
we creep past in silence, winter storm tracking northward

12.09.13

He walks with me down the empty staircase after the last poetry class
not a ghost exactly but a presence I want to believe in, or so I tell him

12.10.13

what I'll miss lies in this
constancy of endlessness

12.11.13

blinking plastic snowflakes strung
suspended from the eavestroughs

12.12.13

The low undertone of a diesel tug
offers its consolation this icy night

12.13.13

In the waiting room rumors of the coming storm
mix with worried whispers about mammography

12.14.13

Yellow cab moving sideways down Seventh Avenue South just past West 4th where
at the subway entrance a man goes down a flight of icy concrete stairs on his back

12.15.13

I have fallen in love with the blemish high on the cheek of the woman in the seat in front of me,
the twists of black hair against her pale scalp, and the way she gathers her things as she leaves

12.16.13

sashimi till déjeuner
pozole ar Abendbrot

12.17.13

The neighbor men lean upon blue and green snow shovels
comparing the icy clarity of the moon and Christmas lights

12.18.13

May they skate so forever, the two angels, alone in the sun tracing ovals on the silver ice
gulls circling overhead and Nat King Cole crooning White Christmas over the rink PA

12.19.13

The student who introduces me to Senryū
teaches me what I've been doing all along

12.20.13

only one tree left hanging among the dangling ropes
this close to Christmas at the deserted garden center

12.21.13

writes on the solstice
a poetic of absence

12.22.13

In the boss's wife's nativity tale she goes into labor the day her sister died;
the baby, *grazie a dio*, born the next day with, *beninteso*, the sister's name.

12.23.13

He asks her if she thinks they are forlorn having only each other as they approach the feast
then thinks of the girl who just ended her pregnancy and wonders how she fares this season

12.24.13

It is enough to have arrived here this eventide
wearied by the ride through the desert night

12.25.13

The infant Christ's tiny, human fingers stretch to caress the nuzzling lamb
but the charge of his touch sends the poor creature bleating from the shed

12.26.13

At a road house in New Jersey whose name recalls Hàn Wǔdì's ode to the celestial horses of Dayuan
pale curves of Chongquin braised fish float to the surface of the white bowl of broth red with hot oil

12.27.13

If you want not to talk we don't have to, he says,
I'm just happy finally to be away from my family.

12.28.13

Briefly nude there as she comes back to bed
Maillol figure in the blue light of morning

12.29.13

darabukka
raindrops

12.30.13

Gathering in reflectional symmetry
shards of a kaleidoscopic holiday

12.31.13

sons, wives and one within
count down to one more

1.1.14

Now nearly a year and three quarters into this two-year sequence
my death seems no more rationally determined, if more inexorable

1.2.14

Outside powdery snow lofts and flares into cockscombs beneath yellow street lamps
while elsewhere icy exhalations of deer bejewel the marsh grass where they bed down

1.3.14

*à la veille de son anniversaire
elle se délecte de la ville enneigée*

on the eve of her birthday
she revels in the snowy city

1.4.14

Mirroring both what and how she sees she
poses before Balthus's "Girl at a Window"

1.5.14

Gazing out from the hotel before we leave, she's caught,
she says, by all the different ways people in the city live.

1.6.14

Epiphany upon the river
a platinotype of icy haze

1.7.14

awaiting the thaw the house
shudders, its pipes choking

1.8.14

voiceless velar stops
oft mark our fucking

1.9.14

Mindless errands of the morning forgotten by noon
Prospero is unable to account for his whereabouts

1.10.14

My oldest friend sends me a poem about meeting Elizabeth Taylor in an elevator fifty years ago writing that he recognized her because her eyes were violet. After that there seems little left to say.

1.11.14

The brume a milky scrim beyond the window where the finches feed
as Ella sings "we'll never, never meet again" Louis' horn cutting in

1.12.14

Processing from the Episcopal church to the yacht club pot-luck after the service
clusters of the funeral goers chat quietly, some holding hands, as the sun appears

1.13.14

The bald eagle circles spread-winged low above a hoary enjambment of jagged floes
 settling next to an oval of lapis open water that seems to float upstream with the tide

1.14.14

Jane's dispatch: "the opposite of a window"
I find myself failing to see through with

1.15.14

its flank rime-glazed, the deer
springs and, leaping, clears

1.16.14

Tonight the firemen go down to the river swarming the ice beneath arc lamps as part of a drill,
in this not unlike the congress of house finches that flitted between the feeders earlier today.

1.17.14

One year, three months, and a day since the storm surge lapsed,
wave patterns swirl in new carpets at the Point Lookout fish shack

1.18.14

The mountain bore the mouse
from Phaedrus forward to this

1.19.14

Having fallen asleep contending with a silent god, he wakes from a dream
where she insists, wrongly, that the verb *remeubler*, to refurnish, is reflexive

1.20.14

That January he began to prepare to set off to the place where he did not think he would be going,
one from which no one returns nor can tell anyone about, he still not believing he was leaving at all

1.21.14

The one who lately awaits, not in ambush, hears but does not speak,
formless yet intimately there, not a shadow but a presence in absence

1.22.14

A delight suffuses us when she returns at day's end and we sit quietly after supper,
candlelight through straw-colored wine casting shades of the oncoming consolation

1.23.14

trying to summon
this namelessness

1.24.14

down the dark well
of what befalls him

1.25.14

Taking shelter from the snow we sit among the young
in the firelight at a wine bar beyond the polluted canal

1.26.14

in the wind the pileated woodpecker
rides the suet cage like a trapeze artist

1.27.14

 Murmurs his only prayer
"Ruach, are you there?"

1.28.14

The five-string banjo has stilled
Beacon Bodhisattva setting off

1.29.14

lunch a sliced Honeycrisp, a handful
of Japanese trail mix, almond croissant

1.30.14

Sometimes I think I am lost *derrière un embâcle*
in the draft of a convent cell this side of death

1.31.14

some sort of disturbance has come over the young women
breath of a zephyr casting a cats-paw upon a pool of sapphire

2.1.14

With the respite in the weather the gents of the hamlet
busy themselves doing chores in their weekend jackets

2.2.14

We leave bed late and come down to toast and the Sunday paper
with its accounts of the death of desire among couples our age

2.3.14

achromatic stasis of windless sky and ice before the storm
single mew gull motionless on a gray piling in still water

2.4.14

what she wants to give she cannot
reluctant to call such wanting love

2.5.14

When the blizzard pauses the squirrel digs a tunnel through the snow to the strewn seed,
starlings force one another off the feeders, and a lone mourning dove struts regally below

2.6.14

leafless black walnut boughs
charcoal shadows on the snow

2.7.14

There are no stories here
that anyone would know

2.8.14

Lying beside her I think that thirty thousand years from now this skeleton, if intact, might clack
in some trackless desert and yet, as she reminds me the poet's wife wrote, "your body, your body"

2.9.14

sat make love lunch afternoon drink dinner out
sun ditto but lunch pasta not soup and dinner in

2.10.14

The river carves an olive channel for itself
meandering through the newly whitened ice

2.11.14

I am waiting for something
that likely has already come

2.12.14

crows among
the whatnots

2.13.14

After a half hour of persistent sleet
its muted tinkling suddenly ceases.

2.14.14

The whole town abuzz in yet another blizzard's aftermath
sharing stories of storms past, snow piled to our shoulders

2.15.14

Little one floats serene in her silent sphere
whither we call to her by her secret name

2.16.14

She smooths her long black hair with white hands,
parts it, braids and unbraids it, lets it down again

2.17.14

All day at intervals caught up in thoughts of ice, its
qualities and extent, margins and mortal significance

2.18.14

The ringmaster retreats to the dark center ring
where none save the aerialist dares venture in

2.19.14

crystal forms grunt in the thaw then fall
sprawling clumped beneath dull shrouds

2.20.14

Foolishly I fear being left behind by what the fellow called Angell calls the squadrons of the dead,
the ones whose fireworks loop impotently from the fires of Kiev, or my lost brother and his friends.

2.21.14

In the forest of the night we construct a castle of smooth barked twigs,
white-tipped fern, frozen moss, and sprigs of bay and winter savory

2.22.14

Called forth by the extravagant warmth of this sunny February Saturday
we circle aimlessly from Connecticut to Connecticut, cold in the forecast

2.23.14

On the last reach toward spring each winter
she invites her furtive neighbors in for brunch

2.24.14

The poodle in the hedge— black, standard bred— wears a wedding gown,
sprichts nur Deutsch, yet pantomimes how it dwells *i measc na leipreacháin*

2.25.14

after his Tehillim
comes sof passuk

2.26.14

So enter we alone now into the octave
preceding his year-ago transmigration

2.27.14

squirrels and bully birds muddle in the perimeter of debris
like us they lack exiguity and so flail and foul themselves

2.28.14

at end, triennially at least, this
most symmetrical of months

3.1.14

For the first time in the year since, he comes to me in a dream, fully alive and fully himself
laughing in a pub, which I fear is in a dream, and reach after him, clutching the empty sleeve

3.2.14

a clown in a *ville lointaine* I rehearsed his dying alone
microwaving a plastic jug of water as a bed warmer

3.3.14

He chalked a rogue horizon
where once there was a wall

3.4.14

Four mourning doves forage the circle of scattered husks
still funerary birds upon which the slate of dusk descends

3.5.14

one day then
you die again

3.6.14

We gather round in tipsy laughter, the pretty fervent girls,
the handsome earnest boys, talking of their poems and yours

3.7.14

ferial nevertheless this inverted last
first holiday has passed into the past

3.8.14

aggregate, laminate, solid surface
give a face to certain of our desires

3.9.14

avoiding this
weary gesture

3.10.14

hemmed in by sin
at the minimum

3.11.14

For awhile we'll live with only this transparent membrane as a ceiling
above which the century-old lungs of the house gasp and contract

3.12.14

The fleeing man dimly reflected in the window
the night the wind blows the door open is me

3.13.14

"Being knowing bliss" is despite appearances palindromic,
sat-cit-ānanda, fruit of the Brahman, sweet taste in its pith

3.14.14

gives himself over to the emptiness
of all that connects him to himself

3.15.14

my ambitions reduced
to these false parallels

3.16.14

dune grass along the cleft
that opens to the freshet

3.17.14

When I was young we stood along the curb on Main Street and waved to the sequined baton twirlers,
Emerald Society pipers, politicians, and platinum-coiffed wrestlers waving back from open Cadillacs

3.18.14

The young poet broods about the "idea of poetry" over Gujarati Thali
while we sit drinking Taj beers beneath the impish gaze of Lord Ganesh

3.19.14

I send the annual spring equinox email a day early
since tomorrow little one makes her way toward us

3.20.14

For now we name you bluet, snowdrop, bloodroot, *iris 'Joyce' reticulata,*
girl gathering blossoms despite winter, spring beauty, dearest Erigenia

3.21.14

Sax man blows slow riffs on "Pure Imagination" along Poets Walk
as avenues away blue eyed Talulla coos softly in her mother's arms

3.22.14

These pretty pictures of her we pass through the aether
burst into flower like meadows beneath Brighid's feet

3.23.14

 "How can you miss someone
you've only known for a day?" JDJ

3.24.14

His ashes were strewn she tells me
along the bed of the stream he loved

3.25.14

Lady Tuilelaith rides out
wearing her berry red hat

3.26.14

The wind whips into scudding cuffs
along the olive drab sleeve of the river

3.27.14

away from these festivities
I try on my funeral suit

3.28.14

En train exactement we await the Maple Leaf
descending from Albany on track three

3.29.14

March ends as it began in disarray, gaskets breaking, the pipe
above the kitchen springs a leak, all arrangements gone awry

3.30.14

The widower sits under a green tent in the Princeton cemetery
gazing past the walnut joinery, the rain, the throng of mourners

3.31.14

back furrow laid
next to the dead

4.1.14

In a ground hold at day's end
taxiway to taxiway fool's mate

4.2.14

To the east a low shelf of leaden clouds slows the ascending sun,
finger of dawn drawing a fiery swath across the murk of the bay.

4.3.14

There is no next
only this now

MICHAEL JOYCE's twelve books include seven novels, most recently *Foucault, in Winter, in the Linnaeus Garden* (Starcherone, 2015) and *Twentieth Century Man* (Seismicity, 2014); a prior book-length sequence of poems from BlazeVOX, *Paris Views* (2012); a mixed collection of media essays and short fiction from SUNY, and two collections of essays on digital media from University of Michigan Press. His pioneering hyperfiction, *afternoon, a story* (Eastgate, 1987) has been translated into French, German, Italian, and Polish and was followed by other electronic works on disk and online. A native of Buffalo, for the last twenty-plus years he has lived along the Hudson River and taught at Vassar College.

Made in the USA
Coppell, TX
02 December 2022